T0401560

UNDERSTANDING ECONOMICS

INFLATION, DEFLATION, AND UNEMPLOYMENT

Laura Loria

Britannica
Educational Publishing

IN ASSOCIATION WITH

ROSEN
EDUCATIONAL SERVICES

Published in 2019 by Britannica Educational Publishing (a trademark of Encyclopædia Britannica, Inc.) in association with The Rosen Publishing Group, Inc. 29 East 21st Street, New York, NY 10010

Distributed exclusively by Rosen Publishing.
To see additional Britannica Educational Publishing titles, go to rosenpublishing.com.

First Edition

Britannica Educational Publishing
J.E. Luebering: Executive Director, Core Editorial
Andrea R. Field: Managing Editor, Compton's by Britannica

Rosen Publishing
Heather Moore Niver: Editor
Nelson Sá: Art Director
Brian Garvey: Series Designer
Tahara Anderson: Book Layout
Cindy Reiman: Photography Manager
Heather Moore Niver: Photo Researcher

Library of Congress Cataloging-in-Publication Data

Names: Loria, Laura, author.
Title: Inflation, deflation, and unemployment / Laura Loria.
Description: New York : Britannica Educational Publishing, in Association with Rosen Educational Services, 2019 | Series: Understanding economics | Includes bibliographical references and index. | Audience: Grades 5–8.
Identifiers: LCCN 2017048062| ISBN 9781538302644 (library bound : alk. paper) | ISBN 9781538302651 (pbk. : alk. paper)
Subjects: LCSH: Inflation (Finance)—Juvenile literature. | Deflation (Finance)—Juvenile literature. | Unemployment—Juvenile literature.
Classification: LCC HG229 .L677 2019 | DDC 332.4/1—dc23
LC record available at https://lccn.loc.gov/2017048062

Manufactured in the United States of America

Photo credits: Cover, p. 1 oneinchpunch/Shutterstock.com; cover, p. 1 (background), interior pages Bluemoon 1981/Shutterstock.com; cover, p. 1 (top), pp. 43-48 (background) bluejay/Shutterstock.com; p. 5 © iStockphoto.com/dusanpetkovic; p. 8 © iStockphoto.com/joephotographer; p. 9 Apic/RETIRED/Hulton Archive/Getty Images; p. 11 © iStockphoto.com/gkrphoto; p. 12 © iStockphoto.com/izf; p. 15 pixelfit/E+/Getty Images; p. 17 Owen Franken - Corbis/Corbis Historical/Getty Images; p. 18 Smith Collection/Gado/Archive Photos/Getty Images; p. 21 Daniel Heighton/Shutterstock.com; p. 22 Encyclopædia Britannica, Inc.; p. 24 Pacific & Atlantic Photos, Inc./Library of Congress, Washington, D.C. (LC-USZ62-123429); p. 25 Library of Congress, Washington, D.C. (LC-DIG-ppmsca-12896); p. 27 Peopleimages/E+/Getty Images; p. 29 © iStockphoto.com/AndreyPopov; p. 30 sanjeri/E+/Getty Images; p. 32 Bloomberg/Getty Images; p. 34 © iStockphoto.com/hoozone; p. 37 © iStockphoto.com/bowie15; p. 38 Boston Globe/Getty Images; p. 40 © iStockphoto.com/Freer Law; p. 41 fstop123/E+/Getty Images.

CONTENTS

INTRODUCTION

Economics, an intimidating word for some, is a social science that studies how a society's resources are shared. The word "economics" describes and analyzes choices about the way goods and services are produced, distributed, and consumed. It also assesses the consequences of those choices. Economic activities devoted to satisfying the primary needs of food, clothing, and shelter are common to all human beings. Economic functions also satisfy people's desire for goods and services that are not essential but that they choose to buy. Such goods and services are often called luxuries, but in most modern countries many luxuries, such as automobiles, television sets, cell phones, and visits to the dentist, are nonetheless considered necessities.

The state of the worldwide, national, and local economies has direct effects on everyday people. Inflation, deflation, and unemployment are parts of an economy that affect how much things cost and how much people have to spend.

Imagine that one day you go to the store to buy your favorite snack, which usually costs $1.49. You have the money in your pocket and can't wait to dig in. When you get to the cash register, the total for your purchase is $2.29. Why does this snack suddenly cost more? How will you be able to afford it if your allowance stays the same or if you lose your after-school job?

If the economy were going through a period of inflation when you went to the store, then that would explain

People must make difficult choices when the prices of goods they typically buy suddenly increase. They may decide to buy less often or not at all.

why the price was higher. Inflation makes goods cost more, which means consumers have to pay more to buy goods. But when things cost more, you can buy fewer things. During periods of inflation, people have to make tough decisions about what to buy. In our snack-purchase scenario, you may have to buy that snack less often, choose an alternative item, or skip snack time altogether.

Deflation, far less common than inflation, is when prices drop. This sounds great in comparison to inflation. Imagine the economy is going through a period of deflation. The price of your snack might drop to $.99, which means you can afford to buy your snack more often. Of course, if the company that makes the snack has to sell its product for less money, it might not be able to afford to employ as many people.

Unemployment is the condition of being without a job. If your parents work at the snack company, and they lose their jobs, you might lose your allowance. Without income, you cannot buy any snacks.

Prices and wages have a direct relationship. When prices go up, as they do in a period of inflation, wages tend to increase as well. From a business perspective, a company should want to pay their workers enough so that they will be able to buy the company's products. In this way, an economy can grow. If prices and wages go down, however, the economy shrinks. Inflation, deflation, and unemployment are parts of the economy that directly impact our financial lives.

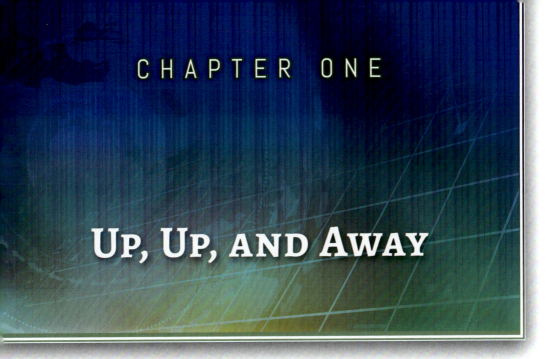

CHAPTER ONE

UP, UP, AND AWAY

You have probably heard adults complaining about the prices of various things going up. Increasing prices seem to be a fact of life. A general increase in prices is called inflation. Of course, prices of selected goods may increase for reasons unrelated to inflation. For example, the price of fresh lettuce may rise because unseasonably heavy rainfall in California has ruined the lettuce crop. Or the price of gasoline may rise if the oil-producing countries set a higher price for oil. During inflation, however, all prices tend to rise.

WHAT CAUSES INFLATION?

Inflation has many causes, but they all operate to raise the demand for goods and services beyond the capacity of the economy to satisfy that demand. Heavy government spend-

Changes in food prices, which are often caused by forces beyond anyone's control, affect people's day-to-day spending.

ing may lead to inflation. Governments can create inflation because they are able to print money. When a government pays its bills by printing money rather than by raising taxes, the demand for goods and services increases. If demand is already high, increasing it will only push up the prices of those goods and services.

The government may not be the only player in the inflation scenario. Citizens, through their voting power, can encourage the government to follow inflationary policies. In the United States special interest groups often exert pressure on Congress for programs that will benefit them at the expense of the treasury. Few taxpayers actually ask their congressional representatives to raise taxes. Government

Germany After World War I

Wartime is often a productive time for an economy. Businesses rush to supply armies with what they need, creating jobs for civilians and putting more cash into circulation. Instead of raising taxes to pay for World War I, Germany borrowed money. Prices rose during the war. The Treaty of Versailles, a peace document signed after they lost the war, required Germany to pay costly reparations. Prices rose again, and the government responded by printing more money. By 1923, the German mark, which had been equal in value to other European currencies, was nearly worthless. There are numerous stories about people filling wheelbarrows full of bills to buy a single loaf of bread, or using money to wallpaper

Massive inflation, such as that in Germany after World War I, can cause paper currency to lose its value. The Rentenmark was introduced to help the nation's recovery.

(continued on the next page)

(continued from the previous page)

their homes, because it cost less than buying wallpaper. People's life savings were now worthless.

Inflation finally halted under new leadership and a new, stable currency, called the Rentenmark. However, the country suffered the effects of an unstable government and economy, which left people vulnerable and angry. This was the perfect time for a new political party to gain new followers and power—the Nazi party.

deficits in themselves do not necessarily lead to inflation, but they make it more difficult to prevent inflation or to slow it down.

Demand-pull inflation is one of the most common types of inflation. In this scenario, the demand for goods is greater than the supply available. Imagine you run a lemonade stand. You only have one glass left, but five people want it. Are you going to charge the same price you've been charging all day, or will you raise it, knowing that someone will pay more? Most business owners would decide to charge more. The next day, when you make more lemonade, you will probably keep charging the higher price, because you know your customers will pay it.

Cost-push is another type of inflation. When the available supply of a good goes down, but there is still a demand for it, prices increase. Natural disasters, such as hurricanes, can cause this type of inflation. If a hurricane ruins crops and causes a shortage of lemons in your area, you would charge more for your lemonade. The increase in prices would help you buy the now more -expensive lemons, which would have to be delivered from farther locations.

Prices fluctuate for all goods, even simple ones like lemonade, on the basis of how many are available and how badly people want to buy them.

People often try to protect themselves from the effects of inflation, which can contribute to rising prices. Consumers want their incomes to increase so as to keep up with rising prices. Rising wages tend to force up prices still further. Those who lend money expect to be paid back in inflation-adjusted dollars. Retired people want their Social Security and other pension payments to increase with the cost of living. As inflation con-

There is a direct relationship between wages and prices—as one increases, so does the other. This can cause problems for those with stagnant incomes.

tinues, people expect it to become even worse and try to compensate for it in advance. The simple expectation of inflation thus helps to keep it going.

PERSONAL IMPACT

Inflation has been defined as "too much money chasing too few goods." As prices rise, wages and salaries also have a tendency to rise. More money in people's pockets causes prices to rise still higher so that consumers never quite catch up. Inflation can go on continuously year after year, so long as the money supply continues to increase.

Continued inflation affects people in diverse ways. Those who live on fixed incomes, or those whose incomes increase very slowly, suffer most from inflation because they are able to buy less and less. Those who lend money when prices are lower may be paid back in dollars of reduced purchasing power. Banks and savings and loan associations generally lose from inflation. People who borrow money, however, may profit by paying their debts in dollars that have shrunk in purchasing power. Inflation thus encourages borrowing and discourages saving. It also leads people to buy real estate and durable goods that will keep their value over time. If inflation continues for a long time, the country as a whole may begin to consume more and invest less as people find it more profitable to borrow than to save. In other words, inflation causes society to use more of its resources for today's purposes and to set aside less for tomorrow's needs.

CHAPTER TWO

PUTTING THE BRAKES ON

How do economists, the people who study economics, know when inflation is getting out of control? When do governments decide to step in and take action to get the economy back on track? There is no one way to identify or deal with the problem of inflation. A variety of methods are used to correct the course of the economy.

MEASURING INFLATION

A price increase on just a few items does not always indicate that an economy is in a period of inflation. There are a few ways of monitoring the prices of items that not only indicate inflation, but also put a number on it. One approach is to deal with a "basket," or selection of goods and services that most people buy. This is the method used in the Consumer Price Index (CPI), compiled by the United States Department

Everyone needs to buy clothing, which makes it a good item to put in the Consumer Price Index "basket" of items that the typical American purchases.

of Labor's Bureau of Labor Statistics (BLS). It is based on the shopping habits of the majority of Americans.

This "basket" includes more than 200 types of items that fall into eight big groups: food and beverages, housing, apparel, transportation, medical care, recreation, education and communication, and other goods and services. These groups cover nearly everything that people buy to meet their needs and wants, based on surveys of around 7,000 regular families. The BLS collects price data on approximately 80,000 goods and services every month and compares that data over months and years. Sometimes, the CPI is called "a cost-of-living index." The CPI increased 1.7 percent, for example, from July 2016 to July 2017.

While the CPI probably is the easiest measurement of inflation for an average person to understand, it is not the only method that the US government uses to monitor the economy. The Producer Price Index (PPI) collects similar data, but this method measures inflation by tracking the revenue that producers receive for their products and services. The PPI usually yields results similar to those of the CPI, so the two methods are often used together. Other measures include the Employment Cost Index (ECI), the Gross Domestic Product (GDP) Deflator, and the BLS International Price Program. One index is not necessarily better than another; together, they give as complete a picture as possible.

CONTROLLING INFLATION

The process of getting rid of inflation is sometimes called disinflation, which means a slowing down of the rate of inflation. Governments around the world have tried a number of methods for slowing or stopping inflation.

Perhaps the most painful aspect of inflation is the measures that must be taken to overcome it. Essentially they involve reducing the pressure on prices. One way is to limit the rate at which the supply of money is allowed to increase. Limiting the supply of money makes it difficult for businesses and consumers to obtain loans; it causes interest rates to rise; and it often creates unemployment.

America in the 1970s

Following the end of World War II, America experienced some of its best economic times. Unemployment was low, wages were good, and the economy was growing. By the late 1960s, however, prices started rising dramatically. Throughout the 1970s and into the 1980s, inflation rates rose significantly, at times reaching into the double digits. Historians call this period the Great Inflation.

During this period, the economy was a disaster. Interest rates rose along with prices, making it difficult to borrow money. The stock market lost value, as people didn't have enough money to invest. Some blame the Great Inflation on oil shortages, government price controls, and the change from gold-backed currency. The nation recovered by the mid-1980s, after a period of recession, or economic downturn.

Gasoline rationing in the 1970s limited how much a customer could purchase, in hopes of ensuring everyone would have at least some fuel.

SUGAR - FLOUR - CEREAL - SPICE

- Store dried foods in tight containers to keep out moisture, insects, dust, and mice.

- Watch out for weevils in hot weather.

CANNED FOODS

- Food in glass should be kept in a cool, dark place. Light affects color, and vitamins.

During World War II, the US government rationed sugar, butter, and other foods and urged citizens to store all food properly to cut down on waste.

FIGHT FOOD WASTE *in the home*

BUREAU OF HOME ECONOMICS
U.S. DEPARTMENT OF AGRICULTURE

Sometimes governments attempt to prevent inflation by making it illegal to raise prices. This works best in wartime when the economy is being organized toward military goals. The United States government used price controls during World War II and supported them by rationing goods that were in short supply. Consumers were given coupons entitling them to buy limited amounts of essential goods in order to make sure that everyone got a fair share. Otherwise lines would have formed outside retail stores and outlets with only those at the head of a line able to purchase what they needed. When controls were discontinued after the war, prices rose rapidly for several years because of the excess purchasing power that had accumulated in consumers' savings. In the early 1970s, when inflation began to exceed 5 percent a year, President Richard M. Nixon established price controls, but the experiment did not work well and was soon discontinued.

Price controls interfere with the free working of the economy. No government regulation can take account of all the complex changes that occur within different industries. Prices of some goods may be falling while those of others are rising; such changes often reflect differences in production costs. The straitjacket of controls prevents the economy from adjusting to such changes in relative costs.

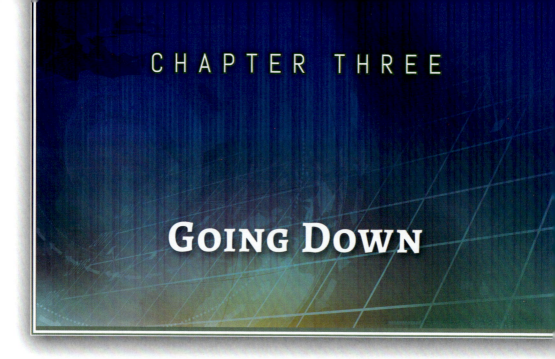

CHAPTER THREE

GOING DOWN

Occasionally, economies have a period in which prices generally go down. This is called deflation, and it is the opposite of inflation. Deflation can occur during periods of recession or depression. Both of these terms describe a period of slow economic activity, with a depression being worse than a recession.

CHEAPER ISN'T ALWAYS BETTER

Low prices sound great, don't they? Unfortunately, lower prices can be a sign of an unhealthy economy. Businesses are less likely to invest in new technology, or try out new products, during a period of deflation. Thus, business-to-business sales decline, and a chain reaction occurs. The slow-down of one type of business, like a consumer goods manufacturer, has an effect on other types, like delivery trucks and stores.

If a company can't charge as much as it used to for a product, it won't be giving its employees raises. Stagnant wages make people nervous. They are afraid that they won't have enough money to afford things in the future, so they stop spending on things they don't absolutely need. Some companies might stop hiring people, or even lay off workers, causing the unemployment rate to go up. When lots of people are looking for jobs, wages go down.

If people lose their jobs, they might not be able to afford their house, car, or student loan payments. They might even default on their debts. When people fall behind on debt payments or cannot pay at all their credit score will go down, making it more difficult for them to get a loan in the future. Banks have to absorb those losses, making them less likely to lend money to others.

Everyone loves to get a good deal, but a series of price drops across multiple industries is a sign of economic trouble.

Which Is Worse: Inflation or Deflation?

So, increasing prices are bad, but decreasing prices are bad, too, right? Inflation and deflation are both signs of change in an economy, which can indicate a trend. Inflation is growth, which can be good for an economy. But, too much inflation can lead to hyperinflation, as in Germany

after World War I. Deflation, however, rarely leads to good economic times. Price reductions across the "basket" in the Consumer Price Index are troubling; they mean that the economy is shrinking, in a way.

In a capitalist society, growth is necessary in order

During Germany's period of hyperinflation, paper money was worth so little it made as much sense to burn it for heat or cooking fuel as it did to buy wood.

to keep the economy running. Businesses get larger and hire more people, who spend more money. That creates the demand for more products. Greater demand inspires people to start new businesses.

Some people wonder if economies can keep growing forever, or if at some point, the system will collapse. History has shown, at least so far, that economies can keep growing, with occasional government regulation to correct their course. Overall, a modest amount of inflation is preferable to any amount of deflation.

THE GREAT DEPRESSION

The Great Depression of 1929 to 1939 began in the United States but spread quickly throughout the industrial world. On October 24, 1929, the complete collapse of the US stock market began; about 13 million shares of stock were sold. The damage worsened on Tuesday, October 29—known ever since as Black Tuesday. More than 16 million shares were sold on this day. The value of most shares fell sharply, and their collapse resulted in financial ruin and panic. Businesses closed, putting millions out of work. Banks failed by the hundreds. Wages for those still fortunate enough to have work fell precipitously. The value of money decreased as the demand for goods declined.

A crowd of people gather outside the New York Stock Exchange on Wall Street in New York City following the stock market crash in October 1929.

By 1932 United States industrial output had been cut in half. One-fourth of the labor force—about 15 million people—was out of work, and there was no such thing as unemployment insurance. Hourly wages had dropped by about 50 percent. Prices for agricultural products dropped to their lowest level since the Civil War. More than 90,000 businesses failed completely.

In 1933, newly elected President Franklin D. Roosevelt began instituting the New Deal, a series of programs designed to turn the economy around and help people. One of the most notable New Deal programs was the Social Security Administration, which provided a monetary support system for the elderly and disabled. He also started the Works Progress Administration, which created jobs for some 8.5 million Americans between 1935 and 1943. Ultimately, the United States' entry into World War II, with the accompanying increase in manufacturing and food production, lifted the nation out of economic crisis.

A poster for the Civilian Conservation Corps, created under Roosevelt's New Deal during the Great Depression, promoted work opportunities in Illinois.

CHANGING COURSE

It is in the government's best interest to take action during a period of deflation, be it a recession or depression. This has become especially apparent since the Great Depression. As a society, America suffered great psychological damage as a result of that period. For decades after the end of the Great Depression, people lived in fear of hunger and homelessness. Although there have been a number of recessions since then, the economy fortunately has not sunk into another depression.

One thing the government can do is to lower interest rates. This encourages banks to lend more and people to borrow more. When people spend that money during a period of deflation, the wheels of the economy start turning in the opposite direction. Businesses make more, so they invest more in technology and employees. More people have jobs, so more people spend money. The economy begins to grow again.

Another government intervention might be to increase its spending in the hopes of stimulating the economy. Governments can offer contracts to private businesses for goods and services or expand their hiring. Both of these methods put more money into circulation.

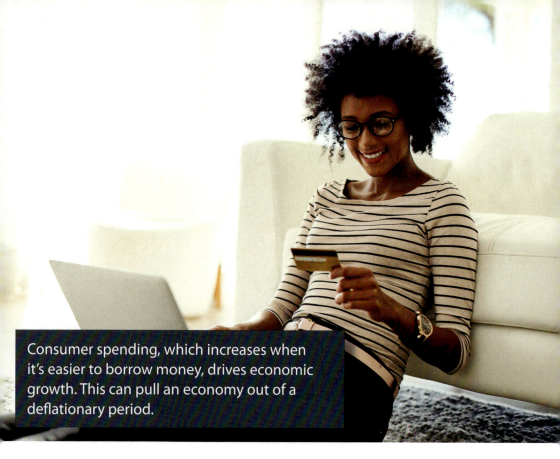

Consumer spending, which increases when it's easier to borrow money, drives economic growth. This can pull an economy out of a deflationary period.

Alternatively, a government might lower taxes or offer tax rebates. This intervention aims to get consumers spending money again, which could get things moving in a positive direction. It is difficult for a government to both lower taxes and increase spending. This increases the national deficit, which makes citizens uneasy.

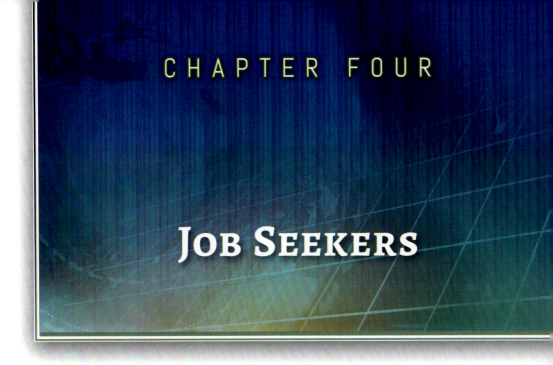

CHAPTER FOUR

JOB SEEKERS

Most people experience the changes in the economy through their jobs. In a good economy, jobs are plentiful and pay well, and raises are consistent. In a bad economy, jobs are harder to find and keep, and pay stagnates or even decreases. The rate of unemployment is one strong indicator of the health of the economy.

WHO ARE THE UNEMPLOYED?

The condition of being without a job is known as unemployment. Specifically, to be considered unemployed a person must be actively seeking a paid job but unable to find one. People who are voluntarily without paid work, such as those who are retired or who stay at home to care for their children, are not called unemployed. Workers may be unemployed because they were laid off or

Not everyone without a job is considered to be officially unemployed. A person must be actively applying for jobs to be considered as such.

fired from a job or because they quit a job. They may also lack work because they just entered or reentered the labor force.

Unemployment statistics do not include everyone who would like a paid job. People who have given up looking for work after a long, unsuccessful job search are not counted as part of the workforce. These people are known as "discouraged workers," and they include workers who have been forced into early retirement.

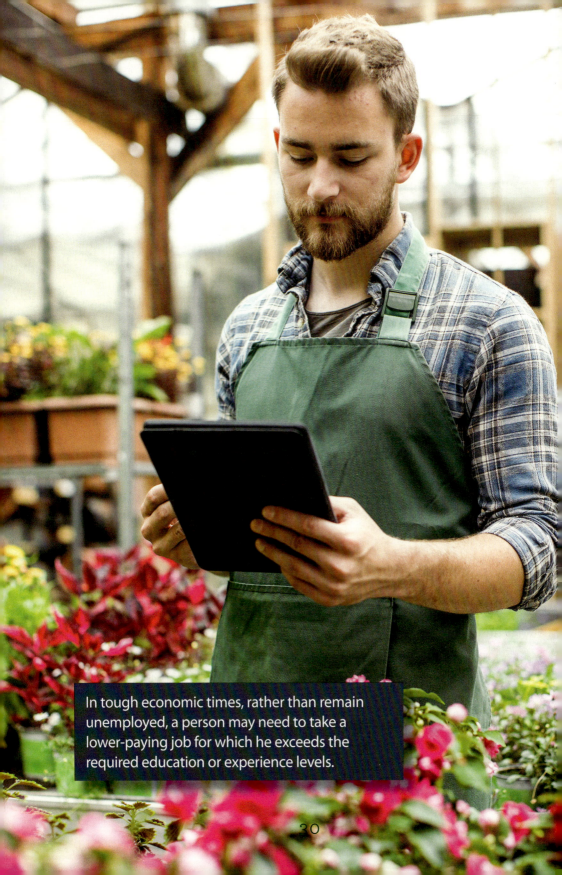

In tough economic times, rather than remain unemployed, a person may need to take a lower-paying job for which he exceeds the required education or experience levels.

People who are "underemployed" are not considered to be unemployed. They would like regular full-time work but are employed for shorter than normal periods. They include part-time, seasonal, day, and casual workers. The term "underemployed" may also describe workers whose education or training makes them overqualified for their jobs. A skilled autoworker who loses his or her job and

The Great Recession and Its Lingering Effect

The US economy experienced a severe economic downturn called the Great Recession from late 2007 until mid-2009. Housing prices fell rapidly, after years of having risen. Most people's biggest asset is their home. When that loses value, they lose wealth. Often, people couldn't sell their homes for enough money to pay off their mortgages, a condition called "being underwater." The home mortgage industry nearly collapsed, and the ripple effect on the rest of the country included the auto industry and the stock market. Approximately two million Americans joined the ranks of the unemployed in the last few months of 2008.

(continued on the next page)

(continued from the previous page)

In the United States, home ownership has been the main source of wealth for many people. The housing crash of the Great Recession plunged many Americans into poverty.

The US government, fearing another depression, decided to lower interest rates and bail out banks and auto manufacturers, investing money to keep them running. The nation's recovery, in terms of jobs lost, took many years. Some feel that the job market has yet to fully recover.

takes a much lower-paying job as a fast-food cashier, for example, is underemployed.

TYPES OF UNEMPLOYMENT

There are three main types of unemployment: structural, cyclical, and frictional. Structural unemployment results from changes in the structure of the economy. Certain industries and types of occupations decline and others grow. As industries shrink, they need fewer workers, and they eliminate positions permanently. People who lose jobs in these industries generally need to find an entirely different type of work.

A second type of joblessness—cyclical unemployment—results from temporary changes in the business cycle. When the economy grows, the unemployment rate is generally low. During recessions and depressions, however, unemployment is high. During such downturns, the overall demand for products and services declines. As demand falls, companies cannot sell as much. The job losses associated with a recession are usually short-term. After the downturn ends and demand grows again, the positions that were lost are often re-created. Structural and cyclical unemployment account for high levels of joblessness.

Joblessness caused by the time it takes workers to find a suitable new job is called frictional unemployment.

Sometimes people lose their jobs through no fault of their own. Larger economic forces can cause an increase in the unemployment rate.

Economies will always have some level of this type of unemployment. Individuals can be unemployed for different reasons. Some people voluntarily leave a job to move, to look for a better position, or for other personal reasons. Other workers are laid off because of restructuring or economic problems at a particular company (rather than across an entire industry or region). Others are fired because of poor job performance. Some of these people will find new jobs quickly; others may not.

CHAPTER FIVE

HELP WANTED

The government has an obligation to help its citizens find and keep their jobs. Simply put, people who work pay taxes and contribute to the nation's well-being. Governments must track employment statistics and support workers, as well as the unemployed. When needed, governments must urge businesses to hire more people.

MEASURING UNEMPLOYMENT

Government labor offices in most countries collect and analyze statistics on unemployment. Analysts study trends in overall unemployment and statistical differences in joblessness between different groups—for example, people grouped by age, gender, ethnicity, occupation, and geographic region. These statistics are studied for what they may reveal of economic trends. The government also uses

To get a clear picture of unemployment trends, data on many factors—such as the gender, race, and age of the unemployed—may be considered in an analysis.

these figures to help determine if it should take action to try to lower unemployment.

Since World War II, many governments have had the goal of achieving full employment and have devised a variety of programs to try to attain it. Full employment does not mean, however, that the unemployment rate is zero. At any given time, the rate will include some people who are temporarily between jobs but who are not unemployed in any long-term sense. An unemployment rate of 3 to 4 percent, for example, is considered quite low. Governments usually try to get the unemployment rate as low as possible without causing too much inflation.

The Fight for $15

Across America, food service and other low-wage workers have engaged in protests over what they feel are unfair wages. The "Fight for $15" movement demands that workers be paid at least $15 per hour. It argues that the minimum wage—$7.25 per hour in 2017 at the federal level (but higher in many states)—is simply not enough to live on. There is a lot of data that supports this argument. In most parts of America, a person making minimum wage cannot afford adequate housing. The protests have sparked change in some places. A total of 19 states increased their minimum wages at the start of 2017, and more states planned to do so later in the year, although most of the wage hikes would not hit $15.

Low-wage workers united in demonstrations across the United States in 2017, demanding higher pay for their labor.

Sometimes government policies intended to protect workers inadvertently contribute to unemployment. Some economists argue that mandating a high minimum wage may increase unemployment by forcing employers to cut back on hiring. In Seattle, Washington, where the minimum wage has been increased steadily, the results have been inconclusive. A 2017 study by the University of Washington claimed that the rise in pay caused workers' hours to be reduced, thereby resulting in them earning less on average. A 2017 study by the University of California, Berkeley, however, found that the minimum wage increases in Seattle had no significant effect on employment.

ASSISTANCE FOR WORKERS

Unemployment insurance is a type of social insurance that pays unemployed people while they look for new work. It is common in developed countries. Benefits are usually paid for only a limited period of time—a period deemed long enough for a worker to find a new job or to be rehired at the original job. To collect benefits, the unemployed worker must be looking for a job and must be out of work involuntarily.

Unemployment insurance benefits vary from one place to another. In most countries the benefits are based

UNEMPLOYMENT INSURANCE APPLICATION

FILING INSTRUCTIONS

Complete this application including any applicable attachment(s). Print or type the information. Use blue or black ink only.

Answer all questions on each page. Review your application thoroughly for completeness. An incomplete application ma[...] delay or prevent the filing of your claim, or cause benefits to be denied. If the Employment Development Department needs to verify any of the information [...] provide while filing a claim, you will receive additional forms by mail and will b[...] asked to provide additional information [...]

APPLICATION QUESTIONS

When people lose their jobs for reasons beyond their control, such as layoffs, they can apply for unemployment insurance to receive income while they search for a new job.

on one's previous earnings. A few countries pay the same amount to everyone collecting benefits. Funding for unemployment insurance also varies from country to country. Employers or employees may be taxed specifically for unemployment insurance, or funding may come out of general government revenues.

Governments can use tax dollars to lower the unemployment rate in many ways. Public spending aimed at stimulating the economy is often called economic stimulus. The government can spend money directly on construction and other public works projects that hire new workers. With their increased incomes, the people hired for these jobs will be able to buy more goods and services.

The construction of a new building leads to employment for the people building it, those who supply the material for the job, and those who will work in it after it's completed.

Demand rises, which thereby helps other industries and their employees.

The government can pay a certain sum to all taxpayers or can increase benefits to such social welfare programs as subsidized housing and food stamps. The government can also offer employment subsidies, or payments to companies that hire new employees.

Changes to taxation rates can also affect employment. Lowering taxes on individuals leaves them with more money with which to buy products and services. Their increased consumption will, in turn, have a stimulating effect on the economy, which can lead to higher employment. Similarly, a reduction in the taxes of corporations stimulates investment. Greater investment leads to an expanding economy and thus greater employment.

GLOSSARY

ANALYZE To study the relationships between different pieces of information.

CAPACITY Ability to perform a function.

CAPITALIST Relating to capitalism, an economic system in which businesses are owned by private citizens and prices are determined mainly by competition in a free market.

CIRCULATION Movement of money from person to person.

COMPENSATE To make up for.

DEFAULT Failure to pay debt.

DEFICIT Having more expenses than income.

DEFLATION A reduction in the volume of available money or credit resulting in a decline of general prices.

DEPRESSION A period of low economic activity combined with high unemployment.

DISINFLATION The act of reducing the rate of inflation.

INDICATOR Information that shows how an economy is doing.

INFLATION A general increase in the price of goods and services.

INTEREST RATE A percentage of money borrowed that the borrower must pay, in addition to the amount of the loan.

INTERVENTION Stepping in to help someone or fix something.

MONITOR To watch over.

RATIONING Limiting the available supply of a good.

RECESSION A downturn in economic activity.

STAGNANT Not active or brisk.

STATISTICS A collection of number data.

STIMULUS An action that causes change.

UNEMPLOYMENT The state of being out of work.

FOR FURTHER READING

Bair, Sheila. *The Bullies of Wall Street: This Is How Greedy Adults Messed Up Our Economy.* New York, NY: Simon & Schuster, 2015.

Brezina, Corona. *Understanding the Federal Reserve and Monetary Policy.* New York, NY: Rosen Publishing, 2012.

Dakers, Diane. *Getting Your Money's Worth: Making Smart Financial Choices.* New York, NY: Crabtree Publishing, 2017.

Furgang, Kathy. *Understanding Economic Indicators.* New York, NY: Rosen Publishing, 2012.

Goodwin, Michael. *Economix: How Our Economy Works (and Doesn't Work) in Words and Pictures.* New York, NY: Abrams ComicArts, 2012.

Hall, Alvin D. *Show Me the Money.* New York, NY: DK Publishing, 2016.

Hamen, Susan E. *The Great Depression and World War II.* Minneapolis, MN: ABDO Publishing Company, 2014.

Hollander, Barbara. *How Deflation Affects You.* New York, NY: Rosen Publishing, 2013.

Levete, Sarah. *The Race to Fix the Global Economy.* New York, NY: Rosen Publishing, 2015.

Meyer, Susan. *Understanding Economic Data.* New York, NY: Rosen Publishing, 2012.

Meyer, Terry Teague. *How Inflation Affects You.* New York, NY: Rosen Publishing, 2013.

Porterfield, Jason. *How a Recession Affects You.* New York, NY: Rosen Publishing, 2013.

Seth, Shaun. *Economics.* New York, NY: Britannica Educational Publishing, 2016.

Sylvester, Kevin. *Follow Your Money: Who Gets It, Who Spends It, and Where Does it Go?* Toronto, ON: Annick Press, 2013.

Weeks, Marcus. *Heads Up Money.* New York, NY: DK Publishing, 2017.

WEBSITES

Bureau of Labor
https://www.bls.gov
Twitter: @BLS_gov

EconEdLink
https://www.econedlink.org/tool/205/Inflation-Video-Quiz
https://www.econedlink.org/tool/202/Employment-Unemployment-Video-Quiz

Social Studies for Kids
http://www.socialstudiesforkids.com/articles/economics/inflation1.htm
Twitter: @SocStudies4Kids

U.S. Inflation Calculator
http://www.usinflationcalculator.com

INDEX